DEVELOPING
CHARACTER
AND CAREER

BRYAN L MCMAHON

BALBOA.
PRESS

A DIVISION OF HAY HOUSE

Balboa Press books may be ordered through booksellers or by contacting:

Balboa Press
A Division of Hay House
1663 Liberty Drive
Bloomington, IN 47403
www.balboapress.com.au
1 (877) 407-4847

Because of the dynamic nature of the Internet, any web addresses or links contained in this book may have changed since publication and may no longer be valid. The views expressed in this work are solely those of the author and do not necessarily reflect the views of the publisher, and the publisher hereby disclaims any responsibility for them.

The author of this book does not dispense medical advice or prescribe the use of any technique as a form of treatment for physical, emotional, or medical problems without the advice of a physician, either directly or indirectly. The intent of the author is only to offer information of a general nature to help you in your quest for emotional and spiritual well-being. In the event you use any of the information in this book for yourself, which is your constitutional right, the author and the publisher assume no responsibility for your actions.

Any people depicted in stock imagery provided by Thinkstock are models, and such images are being used for illustrative purposes only. Certain stock imagery © Thinkstock.

Print information available on the last page.

ISBN: 978-1-4525-2942-4 (sc)
ISBN: 978-1-4525-2943-1 (e)

Balboa Press rev. date: 07/01/2015

CONTENTS

PREFACE

No doubt the first question a reader will ask is, "Why did I consider writing this book?"

Following an early retirement at age fifty-six in 1996 because of the disorder chronic fatigue syndrome, I had to find a pastime that could develop into a passion, as per my medical advice.

As the recommended recuperation action by the immunologist meant a move from Sydney to a quiet environment, we transferred to the Central Coast of New South Wales, and I became committed to lawn bowls. After four years, recuperation was virtually complete, so we made a big decision to move to the Gold Coast.

After seventeen years of total commitment to the sport of bowls, as a player for 7 years and umpire, for 13 years, my wife and I decided a new interest was necessary.

Six years ago, my knowledge of the laws of bowls prompted my involvement in writing technical articles in bowling magazines, which created my appetite for writing.

As I was chairman of the State Umpires Committee I encountered a huge amount of dialogue with members of the bowling fraternity, both young and old, and I became concerned about two sectors of the community. First, a large portion of the younger generation were lost and did not have a plan for life after school. At the other end of the population stream, workers heading into retirement were afraid and anxious about life ahead.

Since my retirement, I had presented my life story to various local organisations, and as the audiences were captivated, I thought I had a story to tell the youth of the day.

A Need for Training

To improve my skills and increase self-confidence, I enrolled in a creative-writing program with the Australian College of Journalism. In addition, I became a member of the University of the Third Age, to participate in a discussion group of fledgling writers.

After the completion of my studies, I commenced the design of the book, which was a three-month project. This timing was essential, because the preparation allowed me to gather confidence, as I knew exactly where I was going.

ACKNOWLEDGEMENTS

I wish to pass on my thanks to all who have given me assistance in my business and personal life, in particular the following:

The mentors mentioned in more detail throughout this book.

All others who gave me guidance.

All my teammates during my sporting life, who convinced me that I had leadership skills.

The training colleges that fine-tuned my skills.

Australian College of Journalism for the excellent training program.

In particular, my wife, who was so patient with my endeavours to develop my career.

My superiors throughout my business life, particularly in London, who had such faith in my potential.

Sincere thanks to two close friends, Susan McAllister and John Butterworth, for their assistance in preliminary editing

INTRODUCTION

What I Hope to Achieve
from This Book

One of my prime goals in business was the development of subordinates. Every time I took an upward movement in my career, a suitable successor was trained and ready to take on the challenges ahead.

Because of this, my aim is to inspire the youth of the world to stand up and be counted every time a challenge or opportunity appears.

On numerous occasions, I took on significant challenges without any doubts, attacked the problems in a considered and aggressive manner, and always sought assistance when necessary.

A considerable factor in my business successes were the mentors in my life, who were always available when I needed guidance to take on my next opportunity or challenge. During the course of this book, I will highlight when and how the mentors assisted.

How do you attract Mentors

- High-quality performance, particularly under stress, will present its rewards.

- It is imperative that emphasis be placed on the key issues in the business.
- If possible, aim to target roles where a high performance can be identified.
- For example, the key issue in the eyes of all business owners is profitability.
- On three occasions, I took on a challenge where the company was operating in a loss situation or trading poorly. There was only one way to go in these circumstances, upwards to success.

As we progress through the book, I will outline examples.

Self-Discipline

Regularly through the book, I will refer to the disciplines I adhered to, and they are all listed at the rear of the book.

I have adhered to a very disciplined life and can remember only two periods of poor discipline, both before I turned thirty years of age.

Listed below are the disciplines that were essential to my development as an individual and in my career. Some of these disciplines were part of my early working life, but many of the more important issues were developed as I gained experience, which included executive development at training colleges. I believe these disciplines will be important to any youth attempting to develop their career:

1. Clearly define your personality, strengths, and weaknesses as soon as possible.
2. Aspire to roles or functions that suit your strengths and personality.
3. Assemble all possible facts and information before making decisions.
4. Avoid making decisions based solely on emotions.

5. Exercise independence when necessary.
6. Identify your career path; don't be overly anxious.
7. Learn how to manage money early in life.
8. Create a plan with objectives for the next ten years.
9. When the objectives have been established, define the short-term links to assist the achievement of the objectives.
10. Determine what training may be required to achieve the objectives.
11. Always be well presented, and when presenting, always prepare well.
12. Take advantage of big opportunities. Don't be afraid of biting off more than you can chew; just "chew like mad."
13. Look after your body. Good diet and exercise—a relaxed mind and a fit body—will allow you to cope with stress.
14. When making decisions for the short term, keep in mind the longer-term goals.
15. When setting long-term goals or making decisions, recognise that the worst possible scenario can occur.
16. Identify individuals who are potential mentors.
17. Identify and train potential successors.

As you work your way through this book, there will be regular reference to these disciplines.

The Mentors' Role in My Life

Mentor Number One, 1968, a Pure Gentleman

When I ventured into the world of insurance brokerage, I became inspired by my first mentor, a man of excellent schooling at Wesley College, a revered and respected college in Melbourne.

He started his working life with an International insurance company and in due course moved through the ranks to manager for the state of Victoria. Obviously, he decided he had greater horizons and formed his own insurance brokerage. The company developed a good reputation, which impressed a large British insurance broker, who purchased part of his company. This opened the International world for my mentor, whilst still maintaining control as managing director.

An acquisition by our London parent company, Matthews Wrightson, in 1971 caused a restructuring of the Australian company, which prompted my appointment as a director at age thirty-two.

My mentor was our parent's representative on the board of directors of the New Zealand subsidiary, and I was briefed on the problems being experienced in New Zealand.

The New Zealand nonexecutive chairman visited Melbourne for detailed discussions, and we quickly developed rapport. He, like I, believed in strong discipline in business, and I agreed to take on the challenge to correct their problems, subject to the acceptance of my wife.

The result was that we flew to Auckland on February 1, 1972.

With hindsight, I realise my first mentor had inspired the inspiration I needed to expand my horizons.

Mentor Number Two, 1975

I greatly respected this Scotsman from Glasgow who spearheaded this International company through dramatic growth, primarily through two large acquisitions in London. This resulted in the company being renamed Stewart Wrightson.

Most insurance brokers in the UK started as family companies, and most had to institutionalise and list on the

London Stock Exchange because of the need for capital to assist growth. In many cases, the family companies lacked suitable candidates within the family to drive the company forward.

Another complication for the company was that almost 50 per cent of Matthews Wrightson was in shipbroking, and advancements in air transport was creating damaging competition.

The board of directors appointed a consultant to conduct a detailed review of the company and to consider possible candidates for the role of CEO of the revised company.

A few years earlier, the company, had purchased my mentor's business in Glasgow. The consultants were so impressed with my friend that they recommended him as the most suitable candidate for future chief executive.

He was obviously impressed with the proposal, but it posed a number of problems. First, his family did not wish to leave Glasgow. Second, he and his wife had a phobia about flying—obviously a problem to be resolved as CEO of an International company. The new CEO travelled Friday night. back to Glasgow, and returned Sunday night. In due course, he and his wife stayed in London most of the time, residing at a magnificent apartment in Whitehall, opposite the Horse Guards.

The first major acquisition of his reign was of Bray Gibb, another family insurance-brokering company; this was considered a coup in insurance markets. A subsequent acquisition of Stewart Smith gave the company increased international exposure, because Stewart Smith had a huge presence in the United States as the world's largest aviation brokerage, thus the change in name to STEWART WRIGHTSON.

The CEOs of all subsidiaries were invited to a London conference, outlining the basis of their business and plans for the future. As I was now managing director of the New Zealand subsidiary, I attended. I explained that as New

Zealand is a small country, the scope for expansion was limited. Notwithstanding, our plan was to be recognised as the most competent and technically equipped in the country, which would lead to a major share of the market.

After dinner on the first night, I returned to my room to find an urgent message to telephone my wife in Auckland. Our non-executive chairman in New Zealand had passed away from a heart attack. As it was impossible to return to Auckland for the funeral, I was on the telephone most of the night, talking to colleagues to ensure there would be adequate representation at the funeral.

I went to the CEO's office at 8:30 a.m. to give him the sad news. After exchanging pleasantries, he asked what we should do to replace the chairman. As I was in London for ten days, I asked for time to think through the options. We agreed to meet again in seven days.

Upon arriving at the CEO's office seven days later, I stated that the past precedent of a non-executive chairman as representative of the owners should continue. However, the two existing non executive directors were not of suitable calibre or market reputation or connections, a sentiment the CEO agreed with wholeheartedly. A candidate with a high business profile was an obvious route.

Our company had grown significantly; therefore, it was time for new blood. The CEO requested my opinion on the resolution of this issue. I then outlined my plan: appointing me executive chairman, on the guarantee that we would secure a new director within six months, of suitable quality to succeed me as chairman within a short period of time.

Knowing I was taking on a huge challenge, I suggested it would be helpful if the CEO or his deputy could visit Auckland for the proposed board meeting, to announce my plan. I explained it would be important that my director colleagues knew of the total support of the London board of directors. The CEO agreed with the plan but requested I carefully plan the proposed discussions with my colleagues.

The CEO said it was necessary to explain to my colleagues that our London superiors had agreed to criteria for the appointment of a new director, including a high business profile. The unqualified support from London gave me the utmost confidence to succeed.

Self-Disciplines Number 3, 4, 12, 16:
Assemble all relevant facts before making decisions; remove emotions from decision-making; identify mentors.

Mentor Number Three, 1975

My first contact with the person who was probably my most influential mentor was in 1975, when I was managing director of the New Zealand subsidiary. He invited me to London for upgraded training and to gain knowledge of the corporate culture and its hierarchy. The superb manner of my introduction to the hierarchy gained me immediate acceptance. He had an indelible effect on my life.

He had endless charm. I will always remember him in Christchurch, New Zealand, sitting on the lounge floor of the local manager's house with the manager's nine daughters, listening to music.

His inner steel assisted the completion of the two major acquisitions in London, because very difficult decisions were necessary—whom to retain and whom to move on. During my trips to London, I enjoyed dining with my friend, because he gave me excellent advice on French wines, such as how to buy the wines at reasonable prices.

A highlight of my first visit to London during 1975 was an invitation to visit their fourteenth-century country house in a village close to Cambridge, which included a visit to Trinity College at Cambridge, where he was educated.

During the late 1980s and 1990s, Lloyd's of London was in turmoil, and most of the insurance market feared for its future. In fact, it looked doomed. My colleague was of the opinion that the future of the insurance market in London was dependent on the survival of Lloyd's of London; therefore, he developed a plan for the future.

My colleague was appointed chairman of Lloyd's, with a brief to implement his plan, which included corporatisation of Lloyd's. The plan succeeded dramatically, and Lloyd's is still a dramatic force in International markets. As a result, my friend was awarded a knighthood.

Later in the book, I will outline how he assisted my development.

Mentor Number Four, 1982

This gentleman became mentor number four when he enticed me to join his company, QBE Insurance in Melbourne in 1982, when I returned from London. His first strategic statement was that we needed to "clear the decks" by improving systems, work practices, and output, thus improving productivity. Also, we needed to improve technical skills. The company still had many "old-time" managers who had not coped with a changing marketplace.

Earlier I talked about my move to this company, which happened as follows. During my trip to Australia and New Zealand, from London, late in 1981, my friend and subsequent mentor advised that his deputy was to visit London, and I was requested to introduce him to senior figures in the London market, i.e., Lloyd's of London underwriters and International insurers. At the end of the deputy's visit, I advised that I was about to resign from the company to return to Australia.

On his return to Sydney, he telephoned to tell me that his superior wished me to join their company as manager for the state of Victoria. I was also introduced to the company's consultant, who confirmed that my long-term friend would continue to press for my transfer to Sydney.

Each month, I was invited to attend the executive meeting, in Sydney to participate in corporate decision-making, a very beneficial process for me. Regularly, he visited Melbourne for ongoing debate about business development and to introduce me to his past contacts.

In hindsight, this was one of my best decisions, because we all excelled in improving the company's performance and dramatically expanding the business.

As a result of an excellent year, in Victoria in 1982, we converted a roughly $3 million loss into a $2 million profit, as a result of increased business and reduced costs. My mentor was so impressed, he asked me to go to Sydney as general manager for Australia. I refused his offer because I had given a commitment to my wife that we would stay put in Melbourne for some years after ten years overseas. I did state that I wished to move to Sydney at some stage in the future and I would indicate when I was ready.

Self-Disciplines Number 3, 12, 16:

Assemble all facts before making decisions; remove emotions in decision-making; and identify mentors when possible.

Mentor Number Five

As mentioned later I moved to the Gold Coast in southern Q'land. In the bowling club, I joined at Paradise Point in year 2000 we had four qualified umpires for club championships, but all had either passed away or become incapacitated, so I was convinced to become a qualified umpire. My trainer into the ranks of umpires became a very close friend.

This sport is very intensive and demanding. Thankfully, this mentor was recognised as a great leader in the bowling community in three Australian states: South Australia, Victoria, and Queensland.

After every day of umpiring, I would discuss the events with my mentor, to determine if I could have handled the issues more competently, in particular my communications with players. The constant involvement with my mentor was of enormous assistance to my development. When I was conducting a training program for new bowlers, my mentor would watch and be ready to suggest improvements.

A level-one umpire is qualified to umpire club championships, a level-two to umpire at district level and at times state championships, and a level-three can officiate at the national or International level. A level-one can apply for level-two qualifications after four years' experience. As part of my training for level two, I was asked to rewrite the training manual in line with the revised international laws.

After my successful completion of the level-two examination, my mentor retired as a member of the district umpiring committee, and I was appointed to succeed him. At that time, my club produced a monthly magazine, and I commenced writing technical articles about the laws of the game.

With two years' experience on the district umpires committee, I was encouraged by my colleagues on the committee, along with my mentor, to apply for a position on the state committee. Following a year's experience, I was appointed chairman of the state umpiring function, which dramatically increased my workload.

Since my appointment as chairman, I became more heavily involved in umpiring state and national events,

Self-Disciplines Number 3, 5, 12, 16:
Assemble all facts before making decisions; exercise independence when necessary; identify individuals as mentors.

The Early Years

My years at primary school were reasonably straightforward, but I remember a few incidents in the last two years.

During my fifth year, in 1949, our class was given a unique experience. We were taken to the Australian Navy quarters at Queenscliffe in Victoria for training, which was my first trip away from home, and I experienced my first hot shower.

My father had always told me to keep out of fights at school, because if you win one, others will wish to challenge. The largest boy in the school, who had been given boxing tuition, was progressively challenging all the bigger boys in the school, so I knew my challenge would eventuate. I watched all his fights and knew that his skills and size would overwhelm me unless I produced something unexpected and quickly.

His boxing stance was traditional—lead with the left—so I took up a traditional stance. But my first move was a straight right to his face with all my power, which pierced his defence and broke his nose. Contrary to my father's advice, I didn't face another challenge during my school years.

Self-Disciplines Number 1 and 3:
If I had not planned for the inevitability, I could have suffered serious injury

Performance at School

Thankfully, my grades during the primary school years were always at the top of the range, resulting in me achieving the "Top of the Class" title in my last year. Inevitably, my father posed the question of secondary-schooling arrangements, and he suggested I enrol at the nearest Catholic college, three suburbs away, where he was educated—a suggestion

I was unhappy with for two reasons. First, the second-best technical college in the state, Footscray Technical College, was only four hundred yards from home; second, I had been linked to the Presbyterian church since my early days.

To gain acceptance to the technical college in those days, it was necessary to qualify by means of an entrance exam, and I lodged an application. I had problems containing my delight when I received a letter from the technical college advising that I had achieved the second-highest mark of the 850 entrants. This achievement entitled me to a coveted scholarship from the local city council, which paid for all costs for the four years, including clothing and excursions.

That evening, after dinner, I asked my parents and grandparents to stay seated because I had exciting news. It was a shock, because I had not advised anyone that I had enrolled for the exam. In particular, my grandmother was over the moon, as she was my greatest supporter. I hadn't advised my parents of my decision, as I didn't want an argument with my father. I knew he would accept my decision if I performed well in the exams.

In hindsight, I realised this was my first lesson in business: a good financial argument will usually defeat a solid philosophical argument.

Self-discipline number 5 applies: sometimes it is necessary to exercise independence.

Teenage Years

Value of Money

During my last year at primary school, the headmaster recommended me to a local pharmacy that was seeking a sensible and responsible lad to assist for two hours after school and three hours on Saturday mornings.

I was delighted, but a snag was ahead. My parents quickly pointed out that as I had a commitment to the food shopping most afternoons of the week, I was unable to accept the job unless suitable arrangements could be agreed within the household.

As I was aware that my sister always sought pocket money from our mother, I put forward a proposal to her: if she'd take over the shopping tasks, I would pay one-third of my salary to her each week.

The job function included sweeping out the premises, restocking shelves, and delivering prescriptions to customers. In due course, the pharmacist trained me to prepare basic medicines, such as aspirin liquids.

Self-discipline number 7 applies: important that the value of money and saving is learnt early in life.

Secondary Schooling

Contrary to my performance at primary school, my academic performance at technical school was inadequate, because I was more interested in sport and earning money. The four years were successfully completed, but the examination results were not flattering. This is one of the poorly disciplined periods I referred to in previous pages.

At that stage, my primary focus was to be a professional footballer.

With the benefit of hindsight, I realised that during those years, I developed leadership skills. First, the members of our sporting team at school appointed me team captain, and second, my teammates at the Footscray junior football team appointed me their leader and captain.

Unfortunately, leadership is a very difficult skill to learn. In most cases, it is inherent in the individual.

SELF DEVELOPMENT

The First Full-Time Employment

I had not resolved the direction I would head forward in my future career, but the engineering teacher was impressed with my adaptability and skill in the fitting and turning engineering classes. The three closest friends of my school days had decided to enlist as apprentice fitters and turners, so I decided to follow suit.

Three of us, at age sixteen, enlisted with the Department of Defence at the ordinance factory in Maribyrnong, which provided the most sophisticated training program known at the time. The training unit was only used by apprentices, and all completed the two-year program before being released to the big, wide world of ordinance equipment.

After twelve months, we were introduced to a personal assessment program, testing intelligence, personality, and leadership skills. I was greatly impressed with this system, because youths don't always make a suitable choice of career, because of a lack of guidance or consultation at school.

After the personal assessment program, which did not have a quantitative assessment, I was advised that the results confirmed I had greater horizons than my career choice. It was suggested that my indentures be terminated, to undertake a career in the administration area, i.e., public service. It was also agreed that I would be rotated throughout the various departments, to gain as much experience as possible as quickly as possible.

Self-discipline number 2 applies: aspire to roles that suit your strengths and personalities.
Early in your business life, you should explore options to identify strengths and personality.

Self-Development

Unfortunately, I did not have access to accurate personal assessments early in my working life, but thankfully, good opportunities came along because of my drive and enthusiasm. Thankfully, as my career developed into the more advanced form of management, I expanded in understanding myself.

My employers pressed for increased management sophistication, and I was enrolled with the Executive Training College, Sydney University, and London Business School. During the training, I was educated in the theories of Myers-Briggs and Carl Jung, and I was assessed as introverted, but not excessively so; thinking; judging.

Thinking, as per the Myers-Briggs formula, means objective, rational, making judgements based on facts, not emotions.

Self-discipline number 1 applies: clearly define your strengths, weaknesses, and personality as soon as possible.

The most dominant trait in my personality has always been thinking, which was extremely helpful when given the task of correcting a nonperforming company or assessing a company as a potential acquisition target. At times, it is inevitable that various paths will cross; in other words, handling exercises that are not akin to our strongest suits.

For example, during my business life, I had to design strategic plans, looking to the future and plotting the future development of the company. Although creative thinking was not my personality strength, I coped reasonably well in these exercises by trying to anticipate what the company should look like in five to ten years and then working back from that point. After completing several of these exercises, I became more comfortable with the process.

Experience showed me that any activity becomes easier after completing it a number of times.

Strengths and Weaknesses

The next exercise was an analysis of my strengths and weaknesses, which will also assist in deciding a career path.

Are you adept with numbers? Do you present well? Are you good with your hands, a good problem-solver, a good team player, or an individualist? Are you a good manager of money, keen on learning other languages, an achiever, a good planner, aware of any leadership skills? The list goes on.

Complete an initial exercise to identity both strengths and weaknesses and constantly review the results. I concluded that expressing myself clearly with clear English terminology was a weakness.

Many students enter part-time work in various industries, which could assist in these exercises.

If you are not numerate, you are not a candidate for accountancy; an introvert would likely fail as a salesman. At one stage in my career, I was selling insurance, and the results were reasonable, because of my hard work, but not top grade because I was fighting against my introverted personality.

Self-disciplines 2, 10, and 11 apply: after identifying the strengths, aim for roles that suit those strengths.

3

Stabilising My Finances

In 1956, at eighteen years of age, I was playing VFL football with Footscray Reserves and being paid a princely sum of thirty shillings a game—three dollars in today's currency. It was an insult, but the club used most of its funds to attract country recruits.

One Sunday morning, I received a visit from Keith Drinan, a previous great from St. Kilda Football Club, who at the time was coach of the Yarraville Football Club, playing in the Victorian Football Association. Keith stated he needed a centre half forward for his club, and he had received numerous recommendations about my ability.

I agreed to train with the club that week and played in a practice match the following Saturday. The next day, I had another meeting with Keith, who offered me a contract paying ten pounds a game. The offer was attractive, because I had a goal to build my first house before my twenty-first birthday. This particular goal was important to me because my parents, since marriage, had always been renters and had not purchased a house.

However, the plan failed when Footscray Football Club refused to grant a clearance to Yarraville based on the recommendation of the reserves coach. I then concluded that the possible gains from football were inadequate to meet my immediate financial goals, and I could supplement my income through other sources. First I took a job cleaning an office block five nights a week; second, I commenced working in a cafe all day on Sundays.

I also accepted that sporting careers have a short lifespan, and I was more interested in achieving my long-term goals: developing myself to play a significant role in industry management or the financial sector.

The next move was to purchase an allotment of land for the construction of my house. As I did not want to overstretch my financial capacity, I limited the cost to six hundred pounds, meaning unmade roads and no sewerage.

I hired a builder after inspecting many of his completed projects and was impressed with the quality of the workmanship. During this period, I was assisted by an uncle who had completed the same process some years before.

Numerous self-disciplines apply: always move forward in areas you are suited for, and never overextend yourself financially.

Change of Direction in Employment

After almost two years in the public service as a clerical trainee, I came to a number of conclusions:

- I learnt nothing during the two years, other than how to spread three days' work into five.
- The work was dead boring.
- There was no challenge.

The thought of me leaving the public service horrified my father.

I started at an insurance company the following week. My new employer, the Automobile Fire and General Insurance Co., was one of the star performers on the stock exchange, and this information changed my father's attitude.

I was totally committed to achieving success, and after a few weeks, I was given a key to the office, because I was always first to arrive. The initial activity was managing the renewal program for the motor insurance portfolio, and after three months, the program was two months ahead of schedule. As a result of my progress, I was then asked to check the work of another colleague who managed the workers' compensation and public liability program.

The next move was to learn about fire, loss of profits, and householders insurance. It was amazing how quickly I absorbed the technicalities of the insurance business. It simply was a matter of spending time on the issues. The performance proved to my superiors that I was there to succeed, and they gave me every opportunity.

Self-discipline number 12 applies: take every opportunity and commit yourself.

After less than twelve months of the rigorous training program, I was invited to the chief clerk's office for a discussion about my next challenge. He enquired whether I would be interested in becoming an inspector—a coveted role as a salesman servicing existing business and acquiring new business in a predetermined geographical area.

My immediate reaction was one of excitement, but I explained that a problem existed, because I did not have a driver's licence. The response from the chief clerk was, "If you are so keen on the role, I am sure you will correct this problem quickly."

Upon returning to my desk, I sought out driving schools. That evening, an instructor arrived at the football club, after my training session, for my first lesson. The next lesson was the following morning, as I drove to the office through the peak-hour traffic, and the lessons continued each morning and afternoon. On the fourth day, I expected another lesson, but the instructor said we had an appointment at the police station at 9:00 a.m. for my driver's licence test.

The state of euphoria as I travelled to the office was amazing, and I rounded off a fantastic morning by displaying my driver's licence when I entered the chief clerk's office. A briefcase was provided, with all the rating manuals and necessary documents, and I was advised that my role as inspector would commence the following Monday and the car would be available on Friday afternoon. The territory to be serviced was to be the Central Business District of Melbourne and inner suburbs of North Melbourne, Carlton, Fitzroy, and Collingwood.

Self-discipline number 12 applies: take every opportunity and commit yourself.

As a new driver, I had to learn quickly to park the car in confined spaces in the inner suburbs. Thankfully, the Volkswagen made life a little easier, but a problem was just around the corner. Whilst turning on a roundabout, the car stopped, and I assumed the petrol tank was empty. The early-model Volkswagens did not have a petrol gauge, and I was unaware that a lever on the floor released fuel from an emergency tank. I pushed the car around the roundabout, and I was terribly embarrassed when the road service mechanic pointed out this issue.

Another amusing incident occurred that was embarrassing at the time. The key priority was to do everything possible to gain the renewal of existing business. Therefore, if a knock at the front door of a residence gained no response, we would go to the rear door. On this particular day, I received the shock of my life when a teenage girl opened the rear door naked.

I continued as an inspector in two metropolitan districts for two years, after which the general manager requested an interview to discuss the next step in my career. My employer's owners, General Credits, a finance company, had purchased a small finance company in Townsville and decided to open a branch; therefore, the insurance subsidiary was expected to do the same. It was determined that, notwithstanding my youth at age twenty-three, I was the preferred candidate to open the insurance branch office.

It was quite a challenge, but I decided to accept the huge demand and head north.

Self-discipline numbers 12 and 14 apply: take advantage of every opportunity; accept the challenge.

The Move North

The challenge was to develop business between Mackay and Cairns from an office in Townsville, meaning travel every second week. Mackay is 250 miles south of Townsville, and Cairns is 250 miles north of Townsville. This posed a huge challenge, because the company did not have a customer in the north, but it helped that General Credits was owned by Commercial Bank of Australia; thus, my first contact in each town was the manager of the bank.

My sources of business were the bank, its customers, and customers of General Credits, which were primarily motor dealers. I found it interesting that the ethnic mix of the population differed from town to town. For example, Mackay had a strong Maltese community; Cairns, Ingham, and Innisfail had very solid Italian communities.

The wet season created many complications, with flooded creeks and rivers, which was exaggerated by poor road systems. In particular, the road systems south to Mackay were the biggest problem, causing me to spend many idle hours sitting on the banks of flooded waterways. One experience—which I laugh about these days—was embarrassing. A notorious creek eighty miles south of Townsville, renowned for flooding, prevented me returning to Townsville. As it was late afternoon, I returned to Ayr to stay at a hotel for the night. The creek was only twenty kilometres north. As I awoke at 4:30 a.m., I decided to go to the creek to determine if I could travel though to Townsville, but the flood showed no sign of abating.

What to do? I decided to return to the hotel for some extra sleep, but as I attempted to mount the stairs to my room, I was confronted by the owner's huge Alsatian dog, which caused me to retreat quickly. Whilst surveying the premises from outside, I noticed that hanging stairs could give access to the upper floor, so I parked my car below the stairs and climbed to the roof of the car to give me access to the hanging stairs. As I mounted the hanging stairs, a police car arrived. Following an explanation, the police officer escorted me up the stairs to my room, because the dog recognised the policeman.

Another interesting experience worth relating involved the managing director when he visited the north. As we headed south to Mackay, torrential rain commenced, and when we reached the notorious road section between Proserpine and Mackay, flood waters had started to accumulate. Because of the poor condition of the road, it was necessary to travel under a rail bridge, but it too was flooded. We drove through the flood, and I could feel the MD's body tense when we reached the deepest point.

Self-discipline number 3 applies: assemble all necessary facts before making decisions.

A frightening experience occurred one morning as I headed to Mackay. About fifty miles from home, I noticed a black flash outside the left-hand side of the car and realised it was the front wheel, which had careered off into a sugar-cane crop. It seemed an age before the front end of the car hit the bitumen, and when that occurred, all I could do was fight with the steering wheel until the speed reduced sufficiently for me to use gear changes to eventually bring the car to a stop.

Thankfully, two young guys travelling in the opposite direction saw where the wheel entered the sugar cane and recovered it. Inside the hubcap were the nuts for the studs, with sufficient thread to allow me to reconnect the wheel and drive—very slowly—the fifteen miles to Ayr, where a customer replaced the front end. At 4:00, I set off on my journey, but by the time I reached the next town of Home

Hill, aftershock kicked in. I could not drive any further, so I stayed the night at the local hotel and had a few drinks and dinner with the local bank manager.

The previous week, the car had been serviced, which included a wheel rotation, and the motor engineers agreed that the most obvious cause of the problem was the possibility that the wheel nuts had not been sufficiently tightened. Thus, they paid the cost of repairs.

Self-discipline number 3 applies: I had decided, after deep thought, that sufficient thread on the studs allowed me to drive further.

Another problem spot was the Herbert River Bridge, north of Ingham, which regularly became flooded because it is probably the strongest-flowing river in the wet season, because of heavy rain in the north of the state. The milk supplies to Townsville were transported from the Atherton Tablelands in huge tankers, and in the wet season, the only way to cross the flooded bridge was to await the arrival of a tanker and follow the tanker across the bridge in its wake.

Self-discipline number 3 applies: accumulate knowledge about the problems you could encounter.

The Value of Knowledge

When travelling up and down the coast, I met many commercial travellers, and I gained vital knowledge from them of all the trouble spots and how to cope with such problems. It reminded me of my Boy Scout training as a teenager and its motto, "be prepared."

Another Change

After four years in the north, the managing director telephoned to say that I was ready for a new challenge and proposed my transfer to Albury on the border of New South Wales and Victoria. I was pleased with this proposal, because Albury Branch was considered the jewel in the crown. A previous manager had been a huge success by developing a fantastic business.

The geographic spread of the business was to Wagga in the north, Benalla and Mount Beauty in the south, Deniliquin in the west, and Corryong in the east. The area is a strong farming community, raising dairy, beef, sheep, grains, fruit, vineyards, hops, and tobacco. North East Victoria and the Riverina are considered some of the best agricultural land in Australia. The area was very affluent, and much business competition continued between towns on either side of the Murray River, Albury and Wodonga. I established many friendships, which still continue to this day.

I was still playing football with reasonable skill when I arrived in Albury, so I joined the Albury Football Club. The club had recruited Murray Weideman, an Australia Rules Football legend, as coach. That year, 1966, we developed an excellent team that won the premiership flag, the first in twenty-five years.

Self-discipline numbers 3 and 12 apply: assemble all the facts before making decisions; take advantage of big opportunities.

Further Albury Experiences

Following the Albury premiership, a friend told me that Howlong Football Club was seeking a coach for the following season. I signed a contract with Howlong, which was an enjoyable experience because of the friendly community of farmers. The small town was on the banks of the Murray River, the boundary between the states of Victoria and New South Wales. I discovered that the club had raised funds for my fee by visiting all farmers in the area to seek support, which was normally a couple of lambs or bags of wheat. We played in the finals for the first time in fifteen years. At the end of the season, the president stated that I was the best coach they had recruited. I was asked to sign a new contract.

Self-discipline numbers 2, 3, and 12 apply: my ability to communicate with players, committee members, and supporters assisted. Be prepared to take on big challenges.

A Further Change in My Life

Whilst in Albury, I decided I wanted greater challenges than conducting business in country areas, even though the lifestyle was heavenly. A Melbourne-based consultant introduced me to two potential employers, an insurance broker and an insurance company. The CEO of the insurance broker advised me that the insurance company, at that stage, was on the market for sale; therefore, the future of the company was uncertain.

Naturally, I joined the insurance broker, and it began a very long-term relationship with the CEO, Frank Strapp, which still exists today, forty-four years later. This company was the Australian subsidiary of a large British company, Mathews Wrightson.

Immediately I was trained to service the needs of existing clients in the construction and civil-engineering industries, property-development sector, and city councils. The most dramatic occurrence, whilst servicing these clients, was when the West Gate Bridge in Melbourne collapsed during construction on October 15, 1970. Unfortunately, thirty-five workers were killed; most were in the workers' huts, having refreshments. We had seven clients working on the bridge at the time but thankfully no casualties. A royal commission found that the collapse was because of inadequate design and an unusual method of construction.

The experience with construction contractors was inspiring, because the civil-engineering clients were becoming involved in some of the more exciting developments in the construction industry—concrete foundations in underground streams for a concert hall. In addition, clients in these industries set very high standards, because errors can lead to fatal injuries, both to employees and the general public.

Self-discipline numbers 3, 5, 11, and 12 apply: be independent; seek greater challenges; present well; and do research about the company you are talking to.

My goal at that stage was to become recognised as a true specialist in advising building contractors and civil engineers.

THE MOVE TO LONDON

The New Zealand Experience

The CEO of the Australian division of British insurance broker Matthews Wrightson was a director of the New Zealand subsidiary representing the London owners. He briefed me on the problems within the New Zealand company. The nonexecutive chairman of the New Zealand company came to Melbourne for discussions about my potential move to Auckland. After a long day of discussions, followed by dinner, I agreed to the proposal, arriving in Auckland, New Zealand on February 1, 1972.

The existing CEO of the New Zealand company had created a huge problem by his overly officious style and procedures that were outside the spirit of the industry agreement. His treatment of the insurance market created anger amongst the senior managers in the industry. At that time, the insurance companies controlled the industry, and an insurance broker needed registration by the controlling body. Because of the anger that had developed, the controlling body advised the New Zealand chairman of our company that they would deregister our company if the CEO was not terminated or replaced.

We retained the existing CEO in a business-development role, which was his great strength, but it was clearly understood he would not be involved in dialogue with the insurance market or general management issues.

After meeting all staff, I expressed delight in the overall quality, but it was obvious they were looking for leadership and direction. My next task was to establish rapport with the insurance market and to explain how we had restructured and how we would operate in the future.

The meetings with the insurance company managers were very successful, and most were keen to develop closer relationships. In fact, some of the managers became close friends. The managers also regarded many of my new colleagues highly.

Issues to Be Resolved:

- The standard of servicing clients' needs appeared quite good, and only fine-tuning was necessary.
- An analysis of our competition was completed.
- We needed to see if we were maximising the use of cash.
- We needed to establish a business strategy.
- We needed to identify my potential successor.
- We needed to consider wider representation throughout New Zealand.
- We needed to establish my credentials in the eyes of staff and the insurance market.

Conclusions:

- My analysis proved that the majority of competitors were spearheaded by executives with huge personalities but lacking in desire to expand their business.
- The bookkeeper who controlled the financial accounts did a marvellous job in using the short-term money markets to earn interest on our cash holdings, between receipt from clients and the date of payment to insurers. However, I pushed for earlier collection

of monies from our clients. Terms of credit became established on the acquisition of the account.

- I identified that all our competitors used a sales technique of focusing on lower premium cost. I advised all staff that our strategy will be to concentrate on advising clients how to maximise the protection of assets, liabilities, and revenue. In addition, we would guarantee very competitive premium cost.
- From my early days, it was obvious that one employee stood out amongst the other staff, but I had plenty of time to confirm this decision on succession. In the meantime, I would do everything possible to develop the individual.
- Development in other cities would be delayed until we had a firmer foothold on the Auckland market. Although Wellington is the capital city of New Zealand, the major business centre is Auckland.

Self-discipline numbers 3, 11, and 12 apply: always assemble facts to impress potential clients; present well; and always aim high.

Establishing My Credentials

My opportunity to prove myself presented itself very early. A year earlier, our company lodged a proposal to the second-largest construction contractor in the country but failed to secure a contract. I studied the proposal prepared by the assistant manager, which I declared amateurish. At that stage, I decided the assistant manager could not meet the standards I required.

I approached the potential client to outline my specialist skills related to their industry. I then explained that my cursory study of their insurance plan had identified serious gaps in protection, particularly in regards to liabilities at law. My statement sent shockwaves through the meeting.

The client asked for my recommendations to correct the problem. I suggested that I would design policies to suit their needs. If accepted by the client, I would sell the proposition to insurers, rather than accept their limited policy wordings. In particular, I stated that we would approach insurers in London who were more progressive than the local market.

After two months of discussions and negotiation, we reached agreement to our appointment as their brokers. Objective achieved.

Self-discipline numbers 3, 11, and 12 apply: do your homework to promote facts to impress potential clients; present well; and aim high.

Future Expansion

From this point, the company surged forward with exceptional growth. To achieve our objectives, it was necessary to expand, which prompted us to open offices in Christchurch and Wellington.

We needed another prestigious customer. A good supporter, the financial director of an existing client, was appointed to the board of New Zealand's largest food processor. I sought his assistance to argue that the company, seeking international recognition, should explore how their international competitors protected their assets, liabilities, and revenue. My suggestion was that the finance director travel to London to talk to numerous international companies.

Our proposal was that the finance director should travel to the United Kingdom at our cost. We would provide accommodations in London at our apartment in Westminster, and our colleagues would introduce him to large international companies. The board of our potential client accepted the proposal, but they preferred to pay the travelling costs.

Our homework told us his wife had a desire to return to Scotland for a visit, and the finance director was a golfing fanatic, so our planned schedule would include provision for these nonbusiness activities. One of our colleagues in London was a member of Wentworth Golf Club, and his house adjoined one of the fairways. The finance director was ecstatic to play on one of the world's most prestigious golf courses. After business was concluded, they completed their trip by travelling to Scotland.

After a very exciting and beneficial two weeks, the finance director dictated his report via Dictaphone and then asked our colleague to arrange typing of the report, which recommended our appointment as their insurance brokers. Of course, we had a copy of the report in Auckland before the finance director returned home. We immediately commenced planning, which would include the opening of an office in Hawkes Bay on the east coast of the north island of New Zealand.

This success shocked the market, because all of our competitors had been trying for years to acquire the account.

Self-discipline numbers 3, 11, and 12 apply:

Our research identified the key factors to swing the deal—personal issues rather than business issues, always present well and take advantage of the big opportunities.

APPOINTMENT OF A NEW DIRECTOR.

Earlier I discussed a dramatic trip to London in 1975, when our New Zealand chairman passed away, and I committed my colleagues to the appointment of a new director, capable of assuming the role of chairman in the near future.

As a result of detailed discussions amongst our directors, we agreed to offer the role to an existing client, Doug Brown, a very successful businessman. Following my meeting with Doug, he accepted the proposal. Doug immediately proved his value, allowing me to resign as chairman, with his subsequent appointment.

Self-discipline numbers 4, 5, 13, and 14 apply: when facing difficult decisions, disregard emotional issues and consider the long term; always maintain good diet and exercise frequently. These principles served me well during this period of great stress.

A Most Dramatic Period for the McMahons

In 1978, we were invited to visit London. I explained to Marilyn, my wife, that the trip was for the benefit of the company, to assess Marilyn as a supportive wife of a potential London-based executive.

One Tuesday night, in early October 1979, Marilyn and I were enjoying a delightful meal at home in Auckland when the telephone rang. To my surprise, it was David Rowland, the company's chief executive. David referred to our discussions during our previous trip to London when he suggested we must shortly discuss the future of my career.

He stated, "The time has come for that discussion," which should take place in his office in London at 8:30 the following Monday morning. Also, he explained that he would expect me to enter into a five-year contract because he was seeking continuity.

Naturally, I sought greater detail about the proposal, but David stated that because of the implications of the proposal, he had to preserve confidentiality. However, he said, "I know you thrive on challenges, but all I can say at this stage is that you'll be confronting the most pressing issue facing the group." David requested a telex the next morning indicating my decision, so he could arrange my transport from the airport if I had decided to go to London for the meeting.

The next morning, I scheduled two meetings, one with our nonexecutive chairman and the other meeting with David, my deputy. During my meeting with the chairman, I outlined the discussion of the previous night with David Rowland. I put forward the possibility of my movement to London, and if so, I wanted his acceptance of David as my successor. As the chairman accepted my proposal, my next move was to talk to David, my deputy.

After I outlined David Rowland's proposal, I told David, my deputy, that if I accepted the London position, I would recommend his appointment as my successor, but only after he had accepted my offer. As my deputy accepted, my next action included arranging flights and accommodation, which entailed an overnight stay in Los Angeles, arriving in London on Sunday morning.

Self-discipline number 3 and 12 apply: assemble the facts and take opportunities.

The Meeting in London

The previous Monday, I received a telephone call from the president of the Insurance Brokers Association from Wellington, to arrange a lunch for Thursday in Auckland, because he had business to discuss. I assumed he wished to discuss industry issues because I was his deputy of the association.

When we sat down for lunch, he stated that their company had decided the future of their company in New Zealand had limited horizons, particularly because of a lack of a suitable successor, as he was in the retirement zone. He proposed that our companies merge and I stay on as managing director of the newly merged group. The proposal had merit, because their company's strength was in Wellington, which was our weakest link.

However, I had to advise my friend that I was flying to London the next day for discussions about a proposal to move to London to confront the company's greatest challenge.

When I arrived at David Rowland's office, he took me to task for opening discussions with a competitor about merging without prior consultation with London—particularly with himself. He completely accepted my explanation outlined in the previous paragraphs. He was aware of the discussions in Auckland, thanks to a telephone call from our competitor's chairman.

The Proposal

David Rowland explained that the Reinsurance Division had an excellent business and technical expertise but had been unable to produce adequate profits. The company was fragmented and overstaffed; it lacked leadership and a future plan. I was offered the position of managing director of the Reinsurance Division, with a brief to establish good management practices, to improve coordination, collective decision-making, and better financial control.

After a briefing of about an hour, we moved to the office of Alan Colls, managing director of the International Division, who produced greater detail, including a copy of the latest financial accounts. He explained that the senior executive of the Reinsurance Division was a superb technician but had no interest in developing management skills. He was only happy when he was in Africa, talking with clients.

Two years previous, an executive had been moved from another division to handle the management and administration, but he failed to produce any results. Alan pointed out that the prior incumbent lacked the strength of character of his colleagues, who were resistant to change. Having listened to all the issues, I suggested to Alan that it must be clearly understood that my appointment was proposed by David Rowland and my direct reporting line was to Alan Colls. My suggestion was accepted by Alan.

The next stage was for me to spend time with the senior executive of the Reinsurance Division. Although he indicated support for the appointment, I was under no false illusions, because in effect, I was given control. We met that night for dinner, and I was sure he was testing my durability.

Before going to dinner I, telephoned Marilyn to outline the proposal, and as expected, she was supportive of the deal—subject to our pets joining us.

Acceptance of the Proposal

The next day was totally committed to agreeing on the basics of a five-year contract. The basics included the costs of selling our property in New Zealand, transportation to London, including the pets, plus the costs of acquiring a property in London. In business decision-making, I have always recognised that the worst possible scenario is a possibility; therefore, I sought agreement from the company to accept the same costs if we needed to terminate the contract and return to Australia.

A very important factor is the possibility of adverse swings in the rate of exchange. Therefore I reached an agreement that in such an occurrence, the company would reimburse us for any rate of exchange loss incurred on funds obtained in London.

Having agreed to all the above issues, I immediately booked a flight to return home the next day, to begin finalising all issues in New Zealand, including installing the succeeding CEO and communicating with the market and customers.

Thankfully, a contract was signed to sell our house the day before our departure.

I am proud to say that I was extremely happy with the task of training David as my successor. Based on the subsequent performance of the company, he responded magnificently to the challenge, and before too long, he had negotiated the purchase of the New Zealand business of the subsidiary of a large Hong Kong-based company.

Self-discipline numbers 3, 11, 12, 16, and 17 apply: assemble facts before decision-making; prepare and present well; always aim high; identify and train potential successors. In this case, I identified my next mentor.

What Is Reinsurance?

Readers may ask, what is reinsurance, and how does it differ from insurance?

The first known form of reinsurance occurred in China centuries ago. Because China is a huge country, it was faced with the problem of moving supplies to the wide expanses of the country; thus, the long, running rivers were the most effective means of delivery. Rather than take the risk of a massive vessel being destroyed by extreme weather or pirates, the Chinese moved supplies in smaller vessels to spread the risk.

The way to profitability in insurance is "spread of risk"; therefore, insurance companies use reinsurance to further spread their risk. In other words, they ensure that no one loss exposes the insurer's balance sheet.

When I joined QBE Insurance in 1982, I was trained to draft strategic plans for implementation, so that our business risk was spread by geography and product.

The biggest challenge was to educate our managers to seek the business that was in line with the company's strategic plan, rather than accept all business offered. A recent example of the need for reinsurance was the 9/11 destruction of the New York World Trade Center. My new employer, a reinsurance broker, was a specialist in advising companies in the developing world. Commonly, these companies didn't have the acumen to satisfactorily analyse the problems within their portfolio. They needed us to advise on methods of protection and to place the reinsurance in international markets. The other problem dealing with developing countries is the fact that their reserve of funds is limited.

Reinsurance is, in fact, the insurance of insurance companies, the spread-of-risk philosophy. Most insurance companies gain their business from direct customers, brokers, or agents, whereas some international insurers gain their business from other insurers. Thus the term *reinsurers,* following the logic of "spread of risk."

The London Experience

Within a month, we discovered a house that suited our requirements and budget at Mill Hill, a largish village nine miles from central London. The village is renowned for an excellent college. The house we purchased was a three-storied Georgian design, a pleasant fifteen-minute walk from the nearest British Rail station.

Marilyn wished to work part time, so she started her search immediately. We were both delighted when she was offered a role as personal assistant to the vice provost at London University College. Her new boss was the foremost expert in atomisation, a forerunner to nuclear activity. In the past, nuclear activity was associated with weapons of mass destruction; however, this power is now being harnessed for commercial and domestic use.

Marilyn enjoyed the role immensely, because she met people of all races and creeds, and she and her boss clicked.

Market Presence

The company's business was well spread, with strong and, in various countries, dominant share of the market. However, its strength was its weakness, because it was lacking a presence in European countries with strong currencies, such as Germany and France. The strongest market position we had in Europe was in Switzerland, which helped the company's cause. Switzerland is one of the most sophisticated insurance markets in Europe and, of course, usually has a strong currency.

Our strongest market share was in Nigeria, because we acted for the National Reinsurance Company. All insurance premiums written in Nigeria by a wide insurance market had to be funnelled into the national body. In Africa, we also had a strong presence in Ghana and Ethiopia. During the later stages of my stay in London, we agreed a plan to develop in French West Africa and, of course, a French-speaking executive was necessary.

In 1980, we recruited a Turkish Muslim to assist our development throughout the Middle East. In Iraq and Iran, we acquired 50 per cent market share of both countries. I greatly respected this man. He was very gentle and kind and hugely committed to his family. In fact, we proposed his recruitment because we knew he wanted to educate his children in England. Our participation in the above countries was logical at the time, because the political scene was reasonably stable, but as I discuss later, the scenario changed dramatically late in 1981.

After the success in Iraq and Iran, our Muslim friend suggested he could acquire the majority of the business in Bangladesh. I was cautious because the past political background had been very turbulent. Different sectors of the community supported varying causes, with most seeking control of the country.

I suggested he present a report to our board summarising the short- and long-term political expectations and outline the financial benefits of such a venture. As I was nervous about the political environment, I was advised that a national constitution had been drafted in 1972. The constitution had been subject to fifteen amendments, so the country was serious about democracy

In due course, our colleague received approval to proceed with his proposal and venture to Bangladesh. I will never forget my meeting with him on his return, when he confirmed that he had been successful in acquiring an order for 100 per cent of the reinsurance business for the country.

However, he explained that we must solve a problem before we can consider the order consummated, because the two senior executives had demanded 10 per cent of our income from the order, to be shared equally between themselves. The problem, he explained, is that his religious beliefs would not allow him to participate in any "bribery."

I agreed to an alternative method of settlement, without involving our colleague, to complete the transaction. Thus, the deal was completed.

Self-discipline numbers 3, 4, and 12 apply: assemble all facts before making a decision; remove emotion from decision-making.

Review of the Company

Notwithstanding the information provided by my superiors, I conducted a detailed review of the company, including its resources, and my findings were as follows: The overriding problems were a lack of

- adequate profitability;
- coordination;
- accountability;
- financial-management skills;
- a discernible culture;
- understanding of the end result in terms of spent capital;
- a clearly defined strategy; and
- flexibility in the use of resources due to leaders' isolationism.

My brief was to teach the organisation to plan, to budget accurately, to maximise the use of resources, and for the board of directors to be collective in decision-making.

Self-discipline numbers 1, 3, and 10 apply: clearly identify your strengths and weaknesses, assemble the facts and determine the training needs of all staff.

Because of the findings outlined above, we agreed to place business development as a low priority, because cost savings must be at the highest priority. Also, the number of youthful staff was excessive but there was no mechanism to determine the individual ability or capacity of the staff.

The most important decisions were as follows:

- When executives travelled overseas, they flew first class, which was amended to economy class, a saving of 150,000 pounds per annum.
- When senior executives of our clients visited London, they were given a Rolls-Royce car, including chauffeur, for their transport, which we downgraded to Jaguars, a saving of 200,000 pounds a year.
- The directors' dining room always served quality French wine for lunch, which we ceased, a saving of 100,000 pounds. We continued to serve quality wines when entertaining customers.
- I programmed a strategic review, involving directors and the assumed younger staff with potential, in order to identify strengths and weaknesses, thus proving information about the capacity of the individuals to develop and showing their developmental needs. The personnel manager worked with me to design the program, so a high degree of demand was imposed on our staff to perform.

The Results of the Project

- The production director for South America had proved that he could acquire business but could not retain customer relationships, which resulted in business losses. In the reinsurance business, the loss of business is expensive, because a company can incur heavy costs after the business is lost for at least ten years. My detailed counselling sessions with the director clearly revealed that he was not interested in servicing. His total focus was in business acquisition.
- As a result of the counselling, the director resigned.
- The most dedicated and aggressive young member of the project teams was seeking a challenge, thus

I discussed with him the South America problem. He was enthusiastic about the challenge, but not surprisingly, he raised the issue of language, i.e., Spanish. My response was to tell him that we had done our homework and had negotiated an arrangement with a college for language training, which guaranteed that a three-month, full-time training program would have him fluent in Spanish.

- Another colleague had been overlooked in the past for promotion, and I was surprised when my director colleagues stated that he was overeducated. During my detailed discussions with this fellow, I discovered he had hidden talents and his fluency in French suited other plans.

- As mentioned earlier, we had a strong presence in Ghana and Nigeria, and it was sensible to consider French West Africa for development. As a result of our deliberations, we appointed him as a production director for French West Africa.

- Six members of the project teams demonstrated reasonable intellect but lacked the drive and commitment to play a significant role in the development of the company. During the next twelve months, the six departed, thus assisting the plans to reduce costs.

- During the early months, I determined that two of the longer-term directors resented my presence; therefore, they were causing disruption. The issues had to be confronted, so I planned my strategy, which included face-to-face confrontation in their own offices, first thing of a morning. The appointment was established the previous afternoon, so they could wonder overnight what I wished to discuss. The first discussion was with the director responsible for Switzerland, who was the most technically equipped in the company and was unpopular for this reason. He was concerned that his colleagues would convince me that he should leave the company, a case of extreme jealousy. I was able to calm his nervousness, and I travelled to Switzerland a couple of times with him. The next discussion was with the director, of Indian descent, responsible for the development and servicing of African business. He had many years of experience in the East African insurance markets. He went to great lengths to emphasise his loyalty to the previous chief executive officer, which meant I had to clearly outline to him my authority imposed by the holdings board. Thus, he would have to work and cooperate with me.

- I started the first board meeting by emphasising the authority vested in me by the chairman of the holdings board. The objective of my role was to instigate structural changes, so that the board of directors would become a coordinated unit, rather than six directors doing their own thing and building brick walls around their individual units. As the holdings board expressed disappointment in the rate of profitability, the key focus during the next twelve months was a severe reduction in costs.

Self-discipline numbers 4, 10, 12, and 14 apply: accumulate facts before decision-making; remove all emotion; and prepare well.

Financial Improvement

Progressively, the directors realised that I would not approve any request for capital expenditure unless the request was supported with a cost/benefit analysis. The improved discipline assisted my cost-saving decisions, discussed earlier, and resulted in a very prompt improvement in profitability. During the first year of my tenure, the pretax profit increased by roughly 5 million pounds, and virtually all the good result came from cost savings.

The following year we received the benefit of a full year's saving on the reduced costs gained the previous year. Additional revenue was produced from new orders in Iran, Iraq, and Bangladesh, which resulted in increased profits of a further 5 million pounds.

Self-discipline numbers 3, 4, and 10 apply: set the objectives; aim high; and stick rigidly to the plan.

Dramatic Events in the Developing World

Political Shift in Iran

When we settled in London, we caught up with a longstanding contact of mine, who was visiting London. He and his family had had a frightening experience in Tehran. My friend was general manager of an American insurance company in Tehran.

In 1979, a push for the return of the Ayatollah Khomeini was growing in strength throughout the country, meaning that the Shah's authority as supreme ruler was being undermined, and his fall from grace was inevitable.

Because of the growing animosity against all things American, our friends were at risk. My friend arranged boarding-school facilities in Europe for their children. The children escaped from Iran on a bus, dressed in Arab clothing. One morning, the "death warning" was painted on their security gate, so our friends put their prepacked cases in the car to head for the airport. They, along with many British citizens, waited two days at the airport until a Royal Air Force aircraft arrived to take all of them to London.

Most readers will be aware the Ayatollah returned to Iran to take total control of the country. The total fabric of the country changed, particularly for academics. Throughout the years, we have met many families who had to flee the country because their fathers were professors at the universities.

In due course, our American friend who was forced to flee Iran was appointed general manager for Austria, resident in Vienna, of an American company.

Conflict between Iran and Iraq

As mentioned earlier, our London-based Muslim colleague was given a 100 per cent order for both countries, being shared with a competitor on a 50/50 basis.

Our Iraqi customers requested that we visit Baghdad, to agree the program for the next year, 1981. Our two production directors' flight was the last commercial flight into Baghdad before the Iranian air force commenced constant bombing of Baghdad. Every morning for the next five days, both parties sat down to talk business, but on each occasion, their intentions were interrupted by sirens advising of aircraft bombing in the next few minutes, prompting all to move to the air-raid shelters.

At this stage, our hosts suggested that progress with discussions was not possible; therefore, our colleagues must leave the country for their own safety. Naturally, the first question was how, because the airport was destroyed by the constant bombing. Our hosts suggested departure by taxi, across the desert to Amman, Jordan, a distance of 806 kilometres. Our hosts asked that my colleagues take with them a lady from Mozambique who was in Iraq on a training program.

The journey was not without problems; halfway through the journey, the taxi broke down. Thankfully, they were close to a mechanic's workshop. However, the mechanic said if Allah said the car could not go, he could not defy Allah. Our Muslim colleague said to the mechanic he would pray to Allah to get his approval. As the mechanic was told that Allah had approved our colleague, the mechanic completed the work which was simply a fan belt replacement.

The drama of the trip continued when they reached Amman because all the hotels were filled to capacity. The trio returned to one of the better hotels, and our Turkish Muslim friend asked for the general manager. Our colleague explained to the general manager that he, like the general manager of the hotel, was a Muslim. Thus, he expected the hotel's general manager to understand the stress, when the general manager was forcing his friend and new wife to sleep on the streets. All of a sudden, two rooms were became available. Whilst all this drama was being enacted, I repeatedly received telephone calls from my colleagues' wives.

Then, out of the blue, our two colleagues walked into our office one morning as if nothing had happened.

Recently, another dimension to this story came to my ears from a neighbour who was a pilot for Singapore Airlines, regularly flying to Iraq. He said he was the pilot of the last flight out of Baghdad when the bombing commenced, and his aircraft passed the Iranian aircraft.

A Nigerian Experience

Nigeria is an interesting country. The British colonised Nigeria during the nineteenth and twentieth centuries, setting up the administration structures, whilst still recognising the traditional chiefs. Nigeria is still a member of the Commonwealth of Nations and became independent in 1960.

The ethnic split is between Muslims in the north and Christians in the south. We acted for most of the insurance companies in the country that were required to remit all premiums from customers to the National Reinsurance Corporation of Nigeria. As we acted for the national company, we controlled almost all business in Nigeria, which was our biggest package of business.

One of our brightest young executives was pushing for international experience, so we agreed to a trip to Nigeria to talk to customers, to determine if he could promote more business. The chief executive of the national company loved stilton, so anyone going to Nigeria took a round of that cheese. Unfortunately, our young colleague, being inexperienced, carried the cheese in his case, which went missing in transit. The cheese finally arrived in Lagos, the Nigerian capital, three days later, after travelling around Africa. When the case was opened by Customs, the stench was unbearable.

One evening, in the Nigerian capital, our colleague was a guest at the home of a customer for dinner, but as he stepped out of the car, he slipped into the drainage channel, which carried all the residents' sewage. It seemed that he had disappeared, because we could not make contact. That was not unusual in Nigeria at that time, because sophisticated, technical communications had not arrived.

His family was distraught because of a lack of news. Within twenty-four hours of falling into the channel, he showed symptoms of serious infection and was locked away in an infectious-diseases hospital. Finally he arrived home safe and sound.

Most of the staff at the National Reinsurance Company of Nigeria were well educated, and when the younger staff visited London, I enjoyed giving them instruction on elementary management techniques. I had similar experiences with the young executives from Ghana.

The Ethiopian Customers

The visits to London by their executives were interesting. Their demands included a nominated quality hotel in the West End, two cases of Scotch whisky, and two cases of gin, plus spending on prostitutes. Naturally, the business discussions were always on the first morning, allowing the rest of their trip for fun.

The Bangladeshi Customers

Earlier, I outlined the terms to acquire their business, but they had no other outlandish requests whilst in London.

Colombia Drama

As mentioned earlier, we arranged Spanish-language training for our most enthusiastic young executive in preparation for his new role as production director for South America. During his first visit, he ran into a difficulty in Colombia, which prompted his call to me late one evening. He was very agitated because of a dispute with our largest client in Colombia.

The client wanted to lodge a claim, even though the premiums had not been paid. Naturally, our colleague stated that the client did not have a claim entitlement until the premium was paid. The client responded by stating that if the claim was not paid within forty-eight hours, the authorities would be advised that he was conducting business in the country whilst on a tourist visa. At length, the client advised our colleague that Colombian jails are not pleasant places.

I arranged a bank transfer, very much against our wishes, which solved the immediate problem. At a later date, we advised the client that in future, we would debit their account on a quarterly basis rather than annually, to prevent further problems.

My Visits to Switzerland

I thoroughly enjoyed my business visits to this wonderful country because the Swiss business world is very organised and disciplined. This explains why the country is so respected by most of the world for its financial expertise and complete confidentiality.

Another good reason for doing business in Switzerland is because their currency is usually one of the strongest in the world. The country can truly be described as central Europe, because it is bordered by France, Germany, Italy, Austria, and Liechtenstein.

Self-discipline numbers 14 and 15 apply: assemble all facts before making decisions.

My Business Trip to Australia and New Zealand

Our two biggest customers in Australia and New Zealand announced that they intended to merge; therefore, it was imperative that I travel south to talk to the hierarchy of both companies in Auckland. My aim was to increase our share of the business but at least retain the existing share.

I flew out of London on Friday evening and arrived in Melbourne on Saturday morning, to spend time with my parents and in-laws. I then flew to Sydney on Sunday afternoon, ready for business on Monday morning.

After two days' business in Sydney, we flew to Auckland for the important part of the trip.

The meetings with our newly merged customers were interesting, and it quickly became obvious that we would retain our share but with no increase. The good news was the merger meant we serviced only one client instead of two, thus reducing our overhead.

The meeting with the new managing director was very refreshing, and we immediately developed a sound relationship. We resumed our relationship twenty-two years later, when retired, and met at our bowling club on the Gold Coast in Queensland.

After the conclusion of all business affairs, I boarded an aircraft in Auckland for the long journey back to London. The journey was dramatic, first because of severe delays in Auckland. Secondly, I missed the connection in Los Angeles to London, meaning I was rerouted to Frankfurt, Germany. Thus the journey took thirty-three hours.

Over the years, I had discovered that future and current problems always became clearer when I was away from normal business on a long flight, and this flight was no different.

The Future

During my trip I came to a number of conclusions.

- I realised I was missing my country of birth.
- Although my stay in London was a success for the company and myself, I did not enjoy the reinsurance business because it lacked true technical skill, and the bribery aspect was distasteful.
- For the above reasons, I didn't see a long-term future for me in the business.
- Through devious means, I was aware that the hierarchy had commenced discussions with potential suitors for either a partial or full sale.
- As we had withdrawn all of the excessive costs from the business, it was ready for an expansion phase.

- I explained earlier that the company had a severe weakness because its business was dominated by weak currencies in third-world countries.

Self-discipline numbers 3 and 4 apply: always gravitate to areas of your strengths; and choose a path to the greater success.

A plan was developed to establish a business base in France and Germany.

The holdings board were delighted with my performance to date and my plan for future development. However, I advised that the development phase into Europe was not my strong suit; therefore, I preferred to terminate my contract and return to Australia to restart my career.

The details of my contract were discussed, and I was asked to prepare the basis of a suitable package to terminate my contract. To my surprise, my suggestions were accepted in toto, and I was asked to stay until April 1, the start of a new tax year. The terms were very generous. The intervening three months allowed me to commence the reorganisation phase of my plan.

Career Alternatives

The holdings board did not wish me to leave the company, suggesting I go to South Africa to resolve massive problems in that market because the local company had been a massive financial burden on the group. The logic was that the role as chief executive in Australia was expected to be available within twelve months.

I rejected the proposal for two reasons, First, the South African business could not be a success because the challenge of changing an Anglicised business to cope with the political and ethnic changes about to take place was too difficult. Thus, the only sensible option was to accept failure and sell the business, but I was not interested in that role. Secondly, history has shown that life is not as predictable as indicated. Therefore, I preferred to restart my business life as soon as possible and rely on my market performance and reputation to secure a suitable, challenging, and financially rewarding role.

When the news of my desire to leave London became known, I received three offers. First, I received an offer as general manager of a company in Hong Kong, but we had no desire to live in Hong Kong. The second was as general manager of an insurance broker in Sydney, but it was not a company I regarded highly. Third, I received a telephone call from a long-term business colleague who had recently been appointed managing director of QBE Insurance, an Australian insurance company that had recently been listed on the stock exchange after being in private hands since its inception. It was agreed that his second in command come to London for detailed discussions about joining the company. After a full day of discussion, I was introduced to their London consultant, who at length explained that although they were delighted for me to join as manager for Victoria, the senior management were expecting me to go to the Sydney head office in the near future.

Both the QBE executive and the consultant requested some evidence of my performance whilst in London, and I supplied a copy of the plan discussed in previous paragraphs, which impressed them greatly. I received an offer letter confirming a start date in April 1982. We returned to Australia following a holiday in Europe, including stays in Paris, Nice, and Rome.

Self-discipline numbers 2, 3, 4, 9, 12, and 14 apply: maintain independence; aim to retain roles that link to your strengths; avoid emotions in decisions, clearly define all short and longer objectives

The Move to Australia

We arrived back in Melbourne early on a Friday morning, and notwithstanding the long flight from Rome, I was quickly into action, buying my wife a new car that afternoon. As we were born and educated in Melbourne, we had a very clear idea of where we wished to live in the future. The next day, we headed off for meetings with real-estate agents.

Our original plan was to rent for a period, to understand the state of the market, but after talking to two agents, we quickly realised that the market had begun an upwards surge, thus our plan changed to purchase mode. One of the agents provided details of all recent sales, and we inspected from the outside four of the sold properties; thus we were ready to proceed.

The agent told us he did not accept conditional contracts—a signed contract for purchase, subject to the sale of another property—however, this was not a problem because my employers in London were required to purchase our London property. Therefore we were cash buyers.

When we entered the agent's car to inspect properties, we were surprised to discover that his car was a gold Rolls Royce. Amazingly, we found a house we fell in love with and advised the agent we would discuss a potential purchase over a cup of coffee. We returned an hour later to indicate to the agent that we wished to sign a conditional contract, which shocked the agent, but he relaxed when we told him the conditions were settlement and possession in twenty-one days. The vendor was surprised by the speed of the transaction but agreed.

The next major task was to locate a suitable golf club for my wife. The task was easier than we expected, and the club was the source of many long-term relationships for my wife. This was important because our absence from Melbourne for ten years meant that many past friendships had evaporated. It was like starting afresh, as was the case in Auckland and London.

Self-discipline numbers 3, 4, 10, 12, and 14 apply: maintain independence; never move to a new role unless it relates to your strengths; assemble all facts, remove emotion from decisions,clearly define all training needs, tackle the big opportunities, and consider the longer term.

DEVELOPMENT OF QBE INSURANCE

The Business Challenge in Melbourne

A brief study of the last annual accounts quickly showed the sheer size of my challenge, a loss of $4 million. As had been the case in previous challenges, the first task was to identify the strengths and weaknesses of the senior managers. It became obvious very quickly that the finance manager's skills were inadequate, and we agreed to his early departure.

I hired consultants with clearly defined criteria, because I wanted the best talent available as finance manager, and I requested our accounting managers in the head office to come to Melbourne to test the technical skills of the candidates. The exercise was a great success, and one candidate had returned to Melbourne after a period as finance manager at the international refugee program in Zurich. When I asked why she had left Australia for Zurich, she very openly stated that it was an "affair of the heart" that fell apart. I was greatly impressed that she had taken me into her confidence, and I promptly offered her the position.

The passing of time proved that it was one of my better decisions. My chosen finance manager, Margaret, was a gem because she was of great assistance in developing performance-monitoring systems that we implemented for all staff. Margaret was still with the company when I retired almost fourteen years later.

Very quickly, it became obvious that most staff had wider horizons than previously demonstrated; all that was needed was support, direction, and leadership.

Setting the Goals

A budget had been prepared by the management team just prior to my arrival, so I reviewed the detail and reduced the expenditure provisions. The management team was given my plan with a request that they complete the same exercise for their area of responsibility and also agree on a goal-setting process with their subordinates.

Known areas of poor performance were given special attention, including weekly monitoring of performance, i.e., work output. When the targets were achieved, an increased target was agreed upon, while the underachievers were counselled and given another time extension. If after two time extensions, a staff member had clearly shown that he or she could not improve, the person's service was terminated. After three months, the staff numbers in the nonperforming areas reduced by 40 per cent whilst at the same time, total productivity increased by 25 per cent. The good performers were rewarded with a salary increase.

Marketing Strategy

The sales manager was given the task of developing a sales strategy, which was product specific; therefore, the sales staff now had a specific sales plan. New business started to flow very quickly, and a greater sense of urgency emerged.

Budget Upgrade

The financial results were ahead of schedule, so the management team agreed to a budget upgrade, which we exceeded at year's end.

First Year's Performance

My original judgement about the management team's quality was proving accurate, and it was also apparent that they responded well to my management style, because the greater sense of initiative and urgency was fantastic.

The financial results at the end of the first year were testament to the previous paragraph, because we had converted a $4 million loss to a break-even position.

Recognition of the Performance

The managing director telephoned one day to compliment the performance and requested I go to Sydney in the role of general manager for Australia. As part of the agreement with my wife to return to Australia, I had committed to staying in Melbourne for a few years.

Therefore, I had no alternative but to reject the offer and agreed to advise when it would be suitable to move to Sydney.

Following this discussion, I developed a plan for the partial decentralisation of the head office by creating two regions, north and south. I proposed that I manage the southern region from Melbourne, the region to include Victoria, Tasmania, South Australia, and Western Australia. The plan was accepted in full.

Self-discipline numbers 3, 4, 5, 9, 11, 12, 14, 15, and 16 apply: acknowledge the big challenge; attack it with vigour; set the objectives; and adhere to the plan; when setting the objectives, recognise the longer term

The Development of QBE Insurance

In May 1981, the board of directors announced the conversion of the former private ownership to a publically listed company on the stock exchange. The company also announced the appointment of John Cloney—an experienced executive with an American insurance company—as managing director. John's experience was vast in all phases of the business in Melbourne, Johannesburg, and New York.

Employees' Participation in the Company's Wealth

During my first year, the boss announced an employee share participation scheme, with each employee's share being dependent on the individual's role in the company. In addition, a bonus scheme was announced, whereby the achievement of goals would be rewarded with extra shares. By the time I retired, I had acquired two hundred thousand shares, either in share issues or bonus shares.

Company Acquisitions

During the first few years, we completed a number of acquisitions, small in size but not posing any major risk to shareholders' capital. Each venture was able to link with the existing business without any major disruption, and we acquired additional expertise. As each piece of business was due for renewal, it was reviewed to determine whether it was within the strict underwriting criteria of QBE. Unfortunately, we incurred a number of losses in the dramatic 1983 bush fires, business that would not have been renewed if renewal had occurred before the bush fires.

Progressively, the acquisitions became larger and with a wider range of geographical spread. A significant development was a reinsurance purchase in Ireland that gave the first presence into the European market. This acquisition also prompted our first influence into Lloyd's of London, which became significant when Lloyd's corporatized because QBE became the largest name in Lloyd's.

Company purchases became the hallmark of our development, and as the years passed by, they included companies in North and South America and Eastern Europe. At its peak, QBE had completed 140 acquisitions throughout the world.

Business Strategy

The business strategy was not ad hoc; all potential acquisitions had to be in line with the business plan, i.e., spread of risk by product and geographic spread and meet our self-imposed goal of producing financial return from the investment within twelve months.

Rationalisation of the UK Business

All overseas operations at that stage were branches of the group, but the board decided that the UK business should be a standalone subsidiary company registered with the appropriate authorities in London. As London is the main centre of insurance throughout the world, it was to be significant in the group's future strategic plans.

I was asked to travel to London for three months to manage the transition and recruit a new general manager. Whilst I was still in London, our new recruit visited Sydney for orientation, and my colleagues in Sydney were pleased with our choice.

Self-discipline numbers 3, 12, 14, and 15 apply: always assemble the facts; don't be afraid to think big; always think of the longer term.

The Result of the Acquisitions

At the time of listing on the Australian Stock Exchange, in 1981, the company had a market value of $30 million, and at its peak, the value increased to $35 *billion,* with a comparative increase in share price from $2.25 to $35.00. Thus, the stock was very popular with investors. I am totally convinced that the share issues to staff were very conducive in creating a great demand for high performance.

THE BUSINESS CHALLENGE IN SYDNEY

The Move to Sydney

In 1987, my wife stated that she was happy to move to Sydney, and I will never forget the drive to Sydney, because it was the day of the stock market crash. The longer we drove, the more the market crashed.

The move resulted in my appointment as assistant general manager—branch operations.

The exercise of buying and selling houses started again. The auction of our house in Brighton was full of drama; the auctioneer faced conducting the auction indoors because of wet weather. Before the auction commenced, the previous owner created a disturbance by announcing that the auction was illegal because we did not have her authority to sell the property. The auctioneer and I were forced to carry her bodily off the premises and threatened to call the police if she attempted to return.

Thankfully, we gained a sale, and in three days, we travelled to Sydney to locate short-term rental accommodation. Awaiting settlement of the Melbourne sale, we had sufficient time to understand the Sydney property market, so we commenced our search for a suitable house in our preferred suburb.

We quickly discovered a house in St Ives on the north shore of Sydney that suited our needs but needed superficial renovation. All it needed was painting internally and externally (totally within my capabilities) and additional drainage. Our choice proved excellent, because we had plenty of common interests with most of our neighbours, many upwardly mobile executives. Also, we were on the edge of a natural reserve, so the bird life was exceptional.

Marilyn established long-term friends at the golf club, and she along with four friends won the pennant championship for the club. Marilyn was playing last, and when she and her opponent walked onto the eighteenth tee, the scores of both teams were equal, but Marilyn won the last hole to secure the pennant championship.

Self-discipline numbers: 2, 3, 9, 12, 14, and 16 apply: gravitate to areas of your strength; assemble the facts; aim big; set objectives, short and long term.

The Business Challenge in Sydney

The work practices and output were poor throughout the company, primarily because our local managers had not moved with the times and were what I termed "1930s managers." My goal was to improve the standards throughout the company that we had developed in Melbourne.

I decided to formalise the business practices, in conjunction with our personnel manager. We moved into a "management by objectives" format. The local managers were required to establish financial-performance goals, in very specific terms, with progressive steps and timeframes to achieve each progressive step. Also, personal-development requirements for themselves and subordinates were required, taking into consideration longer-term career paths.

Progress was monitored every three months, with appropriate counselling when performance did not achieve the predicted result. All staff knew that performance would dictate decisions during the salary-review process. Most of the existing managers responded to the counselling, and the subordinates also improved performance.

Progressively, we identified the managers who could not meet the standards required, and after reasonable time, they were replaced or counselled into retirement. The company had many long-term employees, and quite a number had completed fifty years of service.

I was constantly faced with many difficult circumstances, because very often an employee's wife did not wish her husband to retire. I recall two occasions when I asked husband and wife to come to Sydney for a weekend and join my wife and me for dinner. During one of the dinners, the wife stated "I married my husband for better or worse, but not for lunch."

The difficult cases I encountered taught me that when the husband is still working, there may be a slight crack in the relationship, but upon retirement, the crack becomes a chasm.

In an endeavour to reduce costs, we experimented with new monitoring systems to improve work output, similar to those we implemented in Melbourne. The objective was to reduce the costs at the back end of our business and maintain the expenditure at the front end with customers.

In 1991, we conducted a total review of the Australian business, and I was asked to personally manage all of our associated business, companies for which we had less than 100 per cent ownership. This decision meant I was appointed to the board of directors of an additional six companies that were joint-venture companies. In addition, we entered into ventures with government-controlled businesses, such as Worker's Compensation and Compulsory Motor Third Party.

Self-discipline numbers 3, 4, 12, 14, and 15 apply: assemble all facts; remove emotions from decision-making; aim big; always consider the longer term; recognise that the worst possible scenario can occur.

Government Involvement in the Business

During the 1980s, the state government in Victoria took control of all Worker's Compensation within the state and appointed five companies to act as their agents, but they were bitterly disappointed with the performance of the agents. The authority reopened a tender process for new agents, and we indicated our interest. As our company was regarded as the most efficient manager of the New South Wales system, we outlined our procedures and methods to the decision-makers of the Victorian scheme.

We obviously connected with the officials, because at our next meeting, we were advised that we were to be considered the agent of change, setting the standards for the other agents. We were rewarded with an order for 70 per cent of the total statewide account.

I had commenced discussions with the existing manager of the State Worker's Compensation Authority, and he agreed to join our company if we were successful in our bid for an agency.

The New South Wales government established a compulsory motor third-party injury scheme aimed at providing financial benefits for citizens seriously injured in motor-vehicle accidents. I was asked to join the board of directors of the authority and was subsequently appointed chairman. My key role was communicating with the government ministers.

The major problem was that the parliament was constantly pushing for the widening of benefits, including soft-tissue injuries, which was not the intention of the scheme. It was difficult to explain to the bureaucrats that increasing benefits would increase the cost of the scheme, thus increasing premiums to motorists—a proposal not favoured by the bureaucrats. Finally the only course open to insurers was to advise the government that insurers were considering withdrawing from the scheme, rather than face significant losses.

Joint Ventures

As mentioned earlier, my life changed when I was appointed a director of numerous companies in which we had a financial interest, companies that were specialists in their own field of insurance, as follows:

- aviation
- marine
- travel
- professional liability
- heavy road transport

These joint ventures were a frustration because the partners did not maintain the standard of performance expected of QBE's executives.

One classic example related to the road-transport venture that involved three of our major competitors. An entrepreneur had formed the company and developed a sizable business and then subsequently agreed to sell the company to a joint venture of the three insurance companies. In due course, the venture invited QBE to join, to which we agreed.

Unfortunately, I had very little time to prepare for my first board meeting of the transport insurer. However, I had researched the company's financial results since formation of the joint venture. In each of the four years since inception, the company had incurred a serious loss.

I had a fundamental problem with the structure of the joint venture, because after paying a large volume of cash to the company owner, they appointed him general manager on a generous package. In other words, they had removed his drive to succeed, because he drew his salary irrespective of performance.

The main topic for my first board meeting was a proposal to purchase the company's main competitor, virtually doubling the size of the company. I objected to the proposal because the general manager had failed to perform since the sale, incurring losses each year. Thus, my concern was that the acquisition would lead to increased losses. Also, I argued that the balance sheet of the company could not handle the purchase, because it was loaded with goodwill, which would expand under this proposal.

Whereas my co-directors argued that the purchase would convert the losses into profit, I argued the opposite and stated that any acquisition must produce a return within the first twelve months, and there was no possibility this would occur.

I advised the meeting that I would not sanction the transaction, and in fact I would be reviewing our participation in the venture. A study of the joint-venture agreement showed me that if one partner wished to withdraw, the remaining partners must buy out the departing company's proportionate share. The purchase price would be based on the net asset value at that time, which included a large amount of goodwill. My proposal to our board was to sell the business, which was accepted without reservation.

Self-discipline numbers 3, 4, 5, and 12 apply: assemble all facts; remove emotions from decision-making; aim big with high standards.

MY LARGEST ACQUISITION ACTIVITY IN AUSTRALIA

In 1992, the MD requested I take control of the possible acquisition of the Australian division of a large British insurer. My first task was to know as much about the company as its executives did, and I gave myself four weeks to complete the task, which involved working at their office each weekend. The major objective was to determine whether their business was complementary to ours and if their organisation could be blended into our culture with financial benefits. After completing my exercise, I reported to the managing director by stating that their business could be a very satisfactory add-on to our business and would give further geographical spread and diversification.

One of the investigative teams formed was to determine how their information systems could blend with our systems. The team decided that they could mould the two systems into one; therefore, there was no necessity for two live systems, and thus substantial cost savings.

It was now full steam ahead.

While the financial executives completed all the number-crunching to determine our negotiating point, I prepared strategic and operating plans so that implementation could commence as soon as the cheque was signed. A meeting with all staff of the acquired company was scheduled for 3:00 p.m. on the expected day of settlement, which gave me the opportunity to announce that I had been appointed their new senior executive officer.

I advised that a working team would immediately blend the two computer systems and by means of a budgetary system, we would determine the number of staff needed. In answer to questions from our staff, I confirmed that there would be staff reductions, but it was the intention to retain the best skills available within both companies. I repeated the statement to the staff of the acquired company staff by stating that management would select the best from both companies.

Our decision was to reduce staff numbers at the back end of the business and wherever possible retain existing staff at the front end of the business so that there would be very little disruption to current business and customers.

The Sale Process

The seller had an asking price of $170 million, compared with our starting point of $140 million; following our due diligence, we agreed on $130 million.

An additional team completed a detailed analysis of the liabilities schedule, because I was of the opinion that the liabilities were overstated. Every insurance company installs a reinsurance program as a means of spreading the risk to protect its balance sheet. The acquired company had reinsurance protection for claims in excess of $10,000.

As soon as a claim was lodged with our company and input into our claims system, an entry was entered into our reinsurer's account. Our investigating team discovered that the claims system of the acquired company required the claims staff to create a manual reinsurance entry upon finalising the claim. Our experience had shown that claims staff were very quick to close a claims file on settlement. Therefore a possibility existed that the reinsurance entry could be neglected. We checked every claim over $10,000 and discovered that a large portion of claims had not been lodged with reinsurers, meaning an additional recovery of $10 million.

All branch managers of our company worked with staff of the acquired company to prepare a budget in line with our standards. This process allowed us to identify the actual numbers of staff required and thus the number of retrenchments required. In our drive to reduce costs at the back end of our business, only one member of their head office was retained.

Because my strategic and operational plans were completed by the time of settlement, action commenced immediately. Our MD thought it would be helpful if the general manager of the acquired company could be retained as a consultant, particularly for introductions to the client base. However, he demanded that we should pay him a consultant fee equivalent to his total package as general manager, which I considered excessive. Therefore, we parted ways. As I had the support of their state managers, the absence of their general manager was not a problem.

The venture was a huge success, and we gained a cash return nine months after settlement. The only downside were the physical and mental demands on me. I was away from home for thirty-six consecutive weeks. What pleased me most was that the majority of the staff we wished to retain were still with our company when I retired.

Self-discipline numbers 3, 9, 11, 12, 14, and 15 apply: assemble all facts; set the objectives; present yourself well; aim big with high standards; always consider the longer term.

Illness Forces Retirement

Late in the 1980s, my exercise routine consisted of swimming 1.5 kilometres before work at the North Sydney Olympic pool, which had recorded more world records than any pool in the world. Late in 1994, when I stepped out of the pool, I suffered severe dizziness, prompting me to refer the problem to my doctor. During the following six months, I had three spells off work, but my medical advisers were unable to determine a diagnosis.

By mid-1995, my maximum concentration level on any one subject was approximately thirty seconds. The next step was to consult an immunologist, who after lengthy tests and discussion diagnosed post-viral chronic fatigue syndrome.

The immunologist expressed the problems I faced. The illness was not recognised by the bulk of the medical fraternity. There was no known treatment for the disease and no recognised longevity for it. Her conclusion was that if we did not conquer the disease quickly, I could become a lifetime sufferer—a frightening scenario.

The recommended advice I received was to stop work immediately, move out of Sydney into a quieter environment, and immediately break all past and existing business contacts. I was also advised not to enter the world of personal computers, to identify a pastime that could develop into a passion, and continue constant exercise.

My employers were very helpful, suggesting that I stop work immediately and after three months advise when and if I could return. In the meantime, all my benefits continued unchanged. Our chief executive was aware of the disease because his prior secretary suffered from the same thing and was forced to retire and move to a quieter country environment.

Our GP acquired a report from the United Kingdom, based on 1,500 sufferers of the disease, from a number of universities. The information in the report confirmed the opinions of the immunologist; therefore, prompt action was imperative. The report confirmed that a return to work was not a sensible option, so I had no alternative but exercise early-retirement options. Thankfully, my prudence in a savings plan allowed us to make this difficult decision. In addition, participation in the employer's share plan consolidated our financial position.

The report's summary was a brief statement of the concerns of the sufferers. There were four "hells" to be suffered: the constant symptoms; because the symptoms are internal, no one believes you are unwell; no known treatment; and no finite end to the disease.

Self-discipline numbers 3, 4, 13, and 14 apply: assemble all facts;, remove emotions from decisions; maintain good diet; consider the longer term.

Move from Sydney

Our house in Sydney was immediately placed on the market for sale. In the meantime, we explored options on the Central Coast of New South Wales, and the exercise was assisted by friends who had recently made a similar move.

A few days before the auction of the Sydney house, we discovered a house on the coast almost one hundred miles north of Sydney that adhered to all the criteria we had established. As soon as the paperwork for the Sydney house sale had been completed, we headed for the Central Coast in an endeavour to finalise the purchase of the desired property.

The property was in excellent condition, only five years old, meaning no renovation work, situated on sixteen hundred square metres of land and only three hundred yards from the beach.

Having resolved our housing requirements, the next priority was to gain membership to a golf club for my wife. Friends introduced us to two clubs that my wife fell in love with. Marilyn has never had difficulty in establishing friendships; this was the case at the two clubs, and some friendships still exist.

I decided that my new pastime would be lawn bowls, so I joined the local bowling club at Toukley to commence coaching lessons. In terms of exercise, I still could not swim without adverse reaction, but I was still able to walk the dogs three times a day.

Marilyn's Studies

Our aim was to constantly stimulate our minds. Marilyn had a love of British history, and on advice from one of Marilyn's friends, we enrolled her for the international summer school at Cambridge University. During the first week, the studies were about the Tudor reign—Elizabeth I and her father, Henry VIII. Although Henry was infamous for his many wives, Marilyn was impressed with all the massive changes he implemented, in particular the creation of the Westminster parliamentary system and the formation of the Church of England. He took the dramatic religious decision because one third of all England's taxable income was paid to Rome, and Rome would not agree to his divorce.

The second phase of the studies was about the Stuart Dynasty that succeeded the Tudors. Marilyn was particularly interested in the Stuart regime, because James III was closely linked to the Forbes family, Marilyn's ancestors. The family then constructed the family castle on land west of Aberdeen, which was a castle named Craigevair, not completed by the Mortimer family. The Forbes Dynasty resided in the castle for 350 years before turning the castle over to the National Trust in 1963.

Marilyn was able to experience the unique environment of Cambridge because she lived in Selwyn College, the normal accommodation for full-time students, and lived the life of a full-time student. In addition, the program included live Shakespeare plays in the gardens at night, plus wonderful plays at the Cambridge Theatre. Other Tudor-related marvels were visited, e.g., the Globe Theatre in London and Burghley House in Lincolnshire, the property given by Elizabeth I to William Cecil, her devoted and competent chancellor. The students also visited the castle of Katherine Howard, the fourth wife of Henry VIII.

Independently, Marilyn had visited Hatfield House, the early residence of Elizabeth I, and Hampton Court, the castle constructed by King Henry VIII.

I arrived at Cambridge upon the completion of Marilyn's studies, to travel through England in a manner that coincided with her studies. When we lived in London, I acquired a fantastic manual about all the villages in England. Therefore, during our travels, we only went to villages, bed and breakfasts, pubs, and manors that had links with Tudor times. In Norfolk, we stayed at a bed and breakfast that was a bakery in the early 1500s; the owner was a retired chef and owner of a very prominent West End restaurant.

In Sussex, we stayed at a mansion that housed the prime minister and his military advisers during the Second World War to coordinate the armed forces when defending the south coast of England.

We were staying at a manor in Wiltshire the night Princess Diana suffered a dramatic end. That particular night, we were staying on the estate of Lord Pembroke, a Victorian manor in Wiltshire, and our hostess was emotionally distressed. Because of the dramatic event of the previous night, we visited Salisbury Cathedral, and we were surprised by the magnitude of the sorrow and distress of English citizens.

The following year, Marilyn returned to Cambridge, this time to study the arrival of the Vikings and social change between the two World Wars.

Marilyn was absolutely delighted with her stays at Cambridge, particularly because the tutor at the university, a full-time lecturer of Welsh descent, developed an excellent relationship with her.

My Recovery

After four years, when I told my wife I was now 95 per cent recovered, she immediately suggested a move to the Gold Coast. I had reservations, because when we moved to Sydney, she had difficulty adjusting to the humidity. I suggested we travel to the coast in February to attend the Ladies' Master's Golf Tournament. We could follow our favourite female golfer, Karrie Webb, and give Marilyn the chance to test her reaction to the climate.

The trip was a great success. Karrie broke the course record in the first round and won the event, and Marilyn coped well with the climate. The weather that year was mild; however, Marilyn adjusted after two years. I agreed to the move north, subject to us living by the shoreline, to gain sea breezes and be away from the tourist strip.

After two trips to explore and understand the property scene, we decided on the strip between Paradise Point and Runaway Bay on the coast, which was quickly becoming a retirement zone.

The property agent recommended Runaway Islands, two manmade islands giving direct access to the Broadwater, a magnificent waterways system between the coast and Stradbroke Island.

As soon as the paperwork was completed for the sale of our house, we headed for the Gold Coast, full of excitement. The research we had undertaken earlier was of great value, because we found our dream house within two days. The main reason the estate agent recommended the Runaway Islands was the scope for capital gains in the future, but the very fast growth surprised everyone. The property value increased by 50 per cent within six months.

We quickly organised our sporting interests—a golf club for Marilyn and a bowling club for me—and we were delighted with our choices, because we quickly accumulated solid friendships.

After settling into our new abode on a canal system, we decided to take advantage of the pontoon attached to our property and bought a boat, a twenty-two-foot fibreglass hull, with a 135-HP outboard motor. I loved being on the water with fishing rod in hand when the sun was rising above the horizon. The convenience was unbelievable; I could be in my favourite fishing spot in twenty minutes.

We love our property and its position. Being on an island, we don't have any passing traffic other than traffic related to neighbours. Although the summer can be hot, humid, and wet, the winter is very mild, dry, and very sunny.

Self-discipline numbers 3, 4, 12, 13, 14, and 15 apply: assemble all the facts; aim high with quality and take opportunities; consider the long term, remove emotions and recognise that the worse possible scenario can occur.

My Health during Retirement

As mentioned earlier, I recovered from the earlier illness that forced my retirement, and I was very healthy until I experienced a problem in 2007, at age sixty-eight.

I was umpiring the district's most prestigious bowling tournament, and after nine days of officiating, I became ill with severe dizzy spells. Following an analysis by my doctor, I was referred to a heart specialist for detailed testing, including an ECG. The specialist confirmed that I had experienced two minor heart attacks; therefore, an immediate angiogram was necessary.

The next morning, I arrived at the hospital at 7:00 a.m. to prepare for the angiogram. The specialist stated that the main artery was almost 100 per cent blocked, and another artery was 90 per cent blocked. He advised that he had already consulted with my GP to announce that double bypass surgery was imperative.

The findings were a shock to both my GP and specialist, because all other organs were perfect. The conclusions of the medical advisers was that my problem was genetic, because both of the past two generations of my family died of heart disease in their early sixties. I have never been a smoker, but all of my predecessors were heavy smokers.

At 7:00 the following morning, the specialist telephoned to state that he would conduct the surgery the following morning. I was expected at the hospital at 7 a.m. The surgeon was confident the surgery would be a complete success because of the excellent state of the rest of my body. Also, he was confident that I would not require any additional procedures for at least fifteen years.

The only discomfort I encountered was when I was moved from the constant-care ward and withdrawn from the morphine. The problem was not pain but being in another world.

I returned to umpiring after four weeks but was not allowed to drive for ten weeks, following sign-off by the surgeon. The great concern was the possibility of a collision, forcing my chest onto the steering wheel and opening the wound. At the time of this writing, I have completed more than seven years of recovery without complications, and the specialist only checks me every two years.

The Retirement

At age seventy-five, I have now been in retirement for more than nineteen years and am thoroughly enjoying life. Retirement can be a fantastic experience if your health is good and the financial planning has been effective. The quality of retirement can be directly related to how well you have looked after your body and how well you have planned.

Legislative changes to superannuation during recent years have made a huge difference for retirees. If you plan correctly, preparing for retirement, it is now possible to withdraw funds from superannuation or pension funds without paying tax, provided the limits for other earned income are not exceeded. I have not paid tax for the past ten years, and hopefully the politicians will not amend the existing legislation in the future.

Our retirement has involved constant travel, including three overseas ventures each year and twelve sea cruises.

CHANGE OF INTERESTS AND LIFESTYLE

My Bowling Career

After completing the coaching program at Toukley Bowling Club, I quickly became involved in competitive tournaments, and I was renowned for being on the greens, practising almost every day. Lawn bowls is a technical sport, requiring great skill and touch. Thus, constant practice is necessary, particularly for new bowlers.

The sport is a wonderful way of establishing relationships and is not too physically demanding. It can be played on grass or synthetic surfaces, and different grasses are used throughout Australia, dependent on climate and soil conditions.

The quality of my bowling dramatically improved when we moved to the Gold Coast, because the greens at my new club, Paradise Point, are faster because of the type of grass used in warmer climates. I was pleased to play in every club final other than the open singles, because in the semi-final, I had the game under control against the repeated club champion but allowed the game to slip.

Every year, all districts around Australia conduct pennant tournaments in different divisions amongst the clubs in each district. Each division has eight or ten clubs being represented. Our club enjoyed a good run of success, and I played in two winning teams—the premiership. In one of the wins, I played with three of my closest friends. We were undefeated and won a special medallion because on one end we gained eight shots; our eight bowls were beating all of our competitors' bowls.

Umpiring

Our club had four qualified umpires for club and district championships, but all had either passed away or became seriously incapacitated. Recognising the serious position of the club, I was convinced to proceed with umpiring accreditation.

At the time, our club proceeded with the issue of a club magazine each month, and I designed articles to explain the laws of bowls to our members.

With two years' experience on the district committee, my committee colleagues and John, my bowling mentor, suggested I apply as a candidate for the state committee, which was successful, helped by John's recommendation. Following a year's experience on the committee, I was appointed chairman of the state umpiring function, which dramatically increased my workload.

Since my appointment to the state committee, I arranged and participated in state and Australian championships. After every day of umpiring, I would discuss with John the events of the day, including my decisions, so that he could advise whether my decisions were appropriate or how I could improve next time, particularly the communications with players.

Change of Interests and Lifestyle

After nearly seventeen years of bowling, including thirteen years as an umpire, I needed a change, prompted by the deterioration of a back injury and a need for a fresh impetus.

During my tenure as state chairman of umpires, I regularly visited clubs throughout the state to train potential umpires or umpire state or national tournaments. In addition, I spent endless hours briefing new and older bowlers about the International laws.

When talking to young bowlers, I would enquire about their futures. To my surprise, the majority had no clear plans because of a lack of university qualifications. The ingredients for success are not totally dependent on university education, so I outlined my business successes with only four years of secondary education. However, subsequent education at executive training schools was very helpful.

I concluded that I had now determined my new stimulus, to find a way to assist these troubled souls. Finally, I decided to write an autobiography, designed in the form of a training manual, to show how to be successful without university qualifications.

My life was dramatically influenced by inspirations gained from my mentors; therefore I aim to do similar. How many of the youth can I inspire?

My next big challenge is to decide how to distribute this book to the youth.

CONCLUSION

I have greatly enjoyed this experience, particularly because English was not my strongest suit at school. My career has, in my view, been very successful. Therefore, I have enjoyed a good life through the years. It is not expected that all readers will find the complete writings of value, but I am hopeful that all readers discover information that will assist in future years.

Our world will change dramatically in years to come. First, longevity of life is increasing, and all will be expected to work longer.

My life in retirement has been fantastic because of a healthy body and mind. Most importantly, good financial planning has allowed us to experience wonderful times whilst travelling throughout the world.

I hope many readers will be inspired by this book's contents.

Printed in the United States
By Bookmasters